FATHERS in Austria
Robert Holzer

AF138742

Robert Holzer

FATHERS
in Austria

A forensic autobiographical analysis in
the interest of greater justice

For my children
Susanne and Peter

With love from
your Dad

Bibliographical information of the Deutsche
Nationalbibliothek [German National Library]
The Deutsche Nationalbibliothek [German National Library]
has registered this publication in the German National Bibliography.
Detailed bibliographical data may be viewed at http://dnb.d-nb.de.

Cover design, typesetting, production and printing:
BoD – Books on Demand
ISBN 978-3-7322-7185-6

FOREWORD

This book aims to give information about the situation of separated fathers in Austria. All the life circumstances of this group of people who have suffered curtailment of their rights have one thing in common: as a result of the impossibility of being sufficiently involved in the life of their own children, they suffer incurable wounds which break open again repeatedly and continue to accompany the persons affected until the end of their lives.

In particular I hope to cast light on the role of the state and government authorities as a crucial factor for the law as it is applied in Austria – and it is responsible for multiple mistaken judgments and superficially considered decisions in the area of family law, with far-ranging consequences for fathers and the children.

All the persons involved in these processes of decision (social workers, judges, lawyers and child psychology experts) will I hope read this account attentively. Perhaps they may learn what is happening as a result of their decisions, and happening on a daily basis. Their decisions and judgments are much too short-sighted, and in all cases the consequences will have to be borne by the children.

This book has been created out of the painful experiences of the author, who like many fathers in Austria has lost his children as a result of separation and has been left out in the cold by the responsible authorities in every way.

I would however also like to point to ways of giving the next generation of separated fathers grounds for optimism, for many already find themselves on the road into the abyss, not knowing what they have to expect. Like all before them they too will be broken on the fact that 'modern society' allows them to be reduced to sperm donors and cash cows, a mere source of income – without any right to their children, and without the children having any right to their fathers.

In hope of changing this situation of injustice, the present book may be seen as a *cri de coeur* coming from all suffering fathers – one, it is hoped, that will highlight unfairness, arbitrariness and abuse of the law.

Dr Robert Holzer
Vienna, April 2012

Love of one's own child never dies!

Where personal expressions have been used in this book, they are to be understood as referring to both sexes equally.

Content

Appendix

Chapter I

Marriage and joint custody

We've known each other for a good while by now, we love and trust one another. Everybody says, Why bother to wait? Might as well get married! You two make a really good couple.

Yes, but then there's everything that a marriage involves, what about the marriage contract and all that?

That's something we don't need, it's a bond for life – so why foment mistrust before getting married, and lay down the law about who gets what in case of a separation.

And if it should come to a separation, of course we will deal with it sensibly – not like so many idiots who quarrel over their children and their assets!

No, it's OK, the family is right, you have to do things in the proper form – so let's toddle down to the registry office and testify to our willingness to grow old together and to stand together in coping with whatever difficulties life may throw at us. And Bob's your uncle.

So really and truly, the joyful day dawns, the day of promising always to be there for each other, and all our friends and acquaintances and relations have arrived to congratulate us. What a festive occasion!

So here we are, married, and we want a family – that is to say, we want children!

What is more beautiful than to give the gift of life, and to have the privilege of seeing how the little ones grow up, bringing them up with love and circumspection, preparing them for life as future members of society? We are prepared to take it on, this is something we both want!

The joy of being there at the birth of one's own child, of being sure that the child is healthy, and the tender feeling of connection with the tiny living creature, all these things add up to real happiness.

The business of joint childcare, and their unshakable love of the child, captivates the parents for a long time – and because you don't want your firstborn to be lonely, why not a little brother or sister? So there we are.

The second child arrives, also healthy and enveloped in the same love.

The children grow, and so do the difficulties in the marriage.

Many parents will not see this as being in any way a cause for panic – we can handle it.

At this point in time 'we' still means 'we' – understood as a unit, as a family, as partners with equal rights, who both have the good of their children constantly in mind.

This is what one refers to as 'joint custody', set in stone as a result of the children's having been born in wedlock, unshakable, as long as the marriage is still intact and the children are living in the family home.

Parenthood as a bond for life, unassailable by the state and not offering any loophole for the authorities to intervene. Until separation comes.

Chapter 2

Separation

Separation means dissolution of the life partnership, and is generally deeply traumatic for all the persons concerned. Not only the life partners, but above all the children suffer from separation. No child ever wants its parents to separate! Children will even try, at whatever age, to get the parents to make up, because they don't want to lose either one of them. So parents should feel responsible for bringing about a separation as carefully as possible, always bearing the good of the children in mind.

Unfortunately this is not always possible, and here's where the drama begins.

Separating from your partner naturally involves spatial separation as well.

One of the parents is going to be on their own.

And what about the children?

The children stay with the mother!

And where does this leave the father?

Of course he can see his children when he likes, but first of all you have determine where the children are going to be living. In most cases they will live with the mother, and of course many fathers are quite happy about this – provided that 'joint custody' is established and they can still have regular contact with the children.

In many cases this works OK. But it depends on cooperation on the part of the parent with whom the children are living, and on this parent's making it clear to the children that it is important that they see the parent who is now separated – in most cases the father – on a regular basis.

Divorce means separation of husband and wife, but not necessarily separation of father and child!

This is where the grain comes to be separated from the chaff – in the cases, that is, where the mother will not let the children see the father and/or uses the children as a hostage for getting whatever she wants. This already amounts to child abuse.

But in these very cases, the situation now acquires a new dimension. The fathers panic, they sense the loss they are threatened with, and they too make mistakes – they threaten the mother with the lawyer, the Youth Welfare Office and the court. Blissfully unaware that they are not going to receive any help in these quarters!

The lawyers advise against the father's making a custody application, because they know what the law is. Some lawyers do it all the same, knowing perfectly well that their client is walking into a hornets' nest.

The youth welfare office pretends to be understanding and consoles the father with the argument that you can expect the separation phase to be a bit tricky, because things have not yet been regulated with a divorce settlement and so on and so forth. Once the divorce has gone through things will settle down, it's all going to be all right!

Meanwhile there is already a growing sense of alienation – the children are highly flexible and adaptable, they quickly get used to the new living arrangements.

Many fathers remain unaware that they have already lost everything, that the lawyers and the authorities are lying to them.

In this situation the mothers are already a few steps ahead of the fathers.

As a result of comprehensive 'counselling' on the imminent separation, the wife who is getting ready to divorce will be brought up to speed. She will be shamelessly advised to rip off the father and alienate the children – in the full knowledge that in the present unjust state of the law, the woman can only stand to benefit. But what goes unmentioned is the fact that in many cases this repugnant loading of the scales on the woman's side is going to turn the children into victims as well.

As an example, let me refer at this point to an article in the Österreichische Tageszeitung [Austrian Daily], which read as follows:

'Do you want a divorce? If so, just get on this bus! Put on your bikini, take off your ring! If only it were always so easy to get rid of disagreeables. First aid in all life situations – above all if you are planning a separation or even a divorce – is what the Vienna Women's Bus offers you. Based on the motto "Counselling in places of popular resort", the bus stops at the swimming pool. As well as advice on divorce, the experts on board can give you tips on training and professional opportunities, and information on general legal questions – everything of course strictly anonymous and free of charge.'

The bus displays the logo of the Wiener Frauenhäuser [Vienna Women's Refuges], an organisation which receives subsidies amounting to millions of euros annually from the taxpayer.

It is easy enough to imagine what kind of advice these people give. Certainly not a gentle separation that makes it easy on the child, because this might result in 'disadvantages to the woman'. The brochures and statements emanating from the Women's Refuges radiate hostility – and they lie around as free samples in any 'youth welfare office' – making it quite clear that they are coming from an attitude of hatred of men.

The effects of such counselling is frequently an acrimonious divorce, and there will be interminable legal proceedings at the children's emotional expense. At the cost of the state, in Austria today there are around 400,000 cases of family law registered every year. Nonetheless the Minister of Women's Affairs claims that family law needs no reform. She is, by the way, the one minister in the federal government who – although not formally even responsible! – has been blocking reform of family law in the interest of a fairer deal for the children for years. One wonders why?

Chapter 3

Lawyers

Instinctively fathers sense that something here is out of kilter.

How can it be that the father is suddenly cut off from the information that he crucially needs?

He no longer knows if the children are sick or well, what school they are going to, how they are coping with the new situation. The mother refuses to have any contact with the father – on the advice of her lawyer, because this course of action offers her major benefits; the father gets nervous, misses his children and also goes to consult a lawyer. Definite arrangements need to be made for him to see his children, to keep up contact. The lawyer reassures him that he will see that appropriate arrangements are made, he will appeal to the custody court. Now the divorce industry is fully involved – it is the start of escalation and financial burdens.

And this actually results in a hearing, or negotiation, in the course of which the judge explains to the mother her obligations, but at the same points out, in the presence of all, that in case of any violation of the visiting arrangements he is not going to impose any kind of coercive penalty.

He is the first person who gives the mother to understand that she can do whatever she likes, and nothing is going to happen. He gives her practically *carte blanche*: it is entirely up to her to allow the father visiting rights. The judge has signed off, he has abdicated his own responsibility – which should be to ensure that contact between father and children will not be just at the whim of the mother.

In many cases, of course, it is already perfectly plain what is going to happen: the father becomes a petitioner to the mother, and if it doesn't suit her, he isn't going to see the children.

In other words, the visiting arrangements can be boycotted at any time, without any consequences whatsoever. And so that is exactly what happens.

The lawyer looks into it and informs the father that unfortunately there is nothing to be done, that is just the way the law stands.

In reality, when lawyers represent fathers before an Austrian guardianship court and engage in negotiation on maintenance and visiting rights, they have four opponents: the lawyer of the opposing party, the mother of the child, the expert assessor and the judge!

This is what experienced lawyers say, and the statistics prove them right.

Any lawyer will be happy to represent a mother before the court, because he knows he is bound to win.

So my advice to fathers is this – it would be just as much use to go to court without a lawyer, the result is always going to be the same.

It is just so much money down the drain for putative legal assistance.

Here is what needs to be said to fathers in this situation: Don't fight for your rights, you won't get your rights, your rights are not even worth the paper they are written on.

That is the deplorable state of Austrian justice.

The whistle-blowing function of the state is woefully lacking.

The state legalises the breaking off of contact between fathers and children, and so commits judicial murder of the relationship between the former family members a thousand times over, so damaging the emotions and psyche of the persons involved in a way that goes far beyond the acute loss of a relationship.

The director of the family law division of many years standing at the Austrian Federal Ministry of Justice sums it all up by saying, 'Anyone who fights for his rights with all the resources at his disposal is completely out of line!' and again, 'The UN children's rights convention is just a piece of paper!'

The only conclusion to be drawn from this is that people at the highest level of the state legislature are perfectly well aware, and evidently accepting of the fact that fathers who fight for their parental rights and their obligations to their children have not a chance against the general discrimination.

Not to mention the fact that children's rights are clearly not seen as being important. Even if they are the subject of a UN convention, they have not been recognised by the Republic of Austria at constitutional level in their entirety, or only with 'reservations'.

A perfect demonstration that in the highest echelons of the Federal Ministry of Justice it has long since become clear that the present ghastly state of things is destined to remain unchanged – and thus the daily violation of the law by Austrian local courts, as the responsible court of the first instance in cases of family law, is being swept under the carpet.

Chapter 4

Sole custody

When it has been a good while since the children had any real contact with their father, it is as easy as pie for the mother to put in an application for sole custody.

And with excellent chances that this will be granted without any problem. But this implies, of course, that custody will be withdrawn from the father.

The application will be larded with reproaches and with arguments to the effect that the children don't want to see their father anyway. The best thing, of course, is to make a case for the children's welfare being at risk when they are with their father. The term 'child welfare risk' starts to be used.

This will be either in the form of an expert report (either privately commissioned, or on the order of the court), or through an application by the lawyer, listing in great detail the supposed misdemeanours of the father and at the same time coupled with an application for the suspension of visiting rights, placing the putative risk to the child's welfare squarely in the centre of the frame.

The judge needs these generally spurious reproaches, backed up by the supposed 'child welfare risk', to come to a decision. In fact he gets both in the form of an expert report.

The standard wording of the judgment the mother pursues is that 'A risk to the welfare of the child from the child's father cannot be excluded'. Even in the 'expert report' on the author this formulation occurs – a circumstance that is the more grotesque in view of the fact that the author is a professional paediatrician.

But with that the judge is let off the hook – he can now appeal to the expert report which he has commissioned in hope of receiving a clear recommendation.

Contesting these prejudicial expert reports is *de facto* not an option.

Expert reports arguing the father's case will generally be thrown out. Higher level expert reports are virtually never asked for.

So the kidnapping becomes legal.

The mother creates the children's new life circumstances, the court gives its approval and the question of the child's welfare is not discussed.

The judge puts the wishes of the mother above the law.

This is because in the eyes of the law the pre-eminent objective is supposed to be joint custody, and the courts are meant to explore all possible avenues with a view to reaching it.

In reality, however, the court does nothing whatever to this end, simply confirming in response to a simple application 'the transfer of sole custody to the mother'.

What this means is something the affected fathers have yet to learn.

Until we come to the first incidents involving kindergarten, school or hospital.

Then, you see, the father is suddenly going to be viewed as an intrusive third party. He will not be given information. And it will be pointed out to him that he is actually a nobody. School, kindergarten and sports clubs have been instructed by the mother that the father has no custody, and that he only makes disturbance and difficulties. Woe betide him if he lets them catch a glimpse of him. The Mothers' Welfare Office (commonly known as the Youth Welfare Office) will be notified immediately and informed that the father is 'harassing', 'stalking', 'intimidating', 'frightening', 'upsetting' and 'spying on' the children.

This is the first time most fathers become aware of what it means to be deprived of custody.

Everything that was formerly taken for granted is now denied to the father. He has been sent into exile.

He begins to sense what the term *Zahlvater* means – to be a father who is no more than a source of financial support, a cash cow.

He has been deprived of his rights, but his obligation to pay maintenance is something brought home to him every month, backed up by the threat of compulsory enforcement.

He is not allowed to be a father any more.

It is an organised crime, involving abuse of the legal situation and contempt of the fundamental principle of equality, to establish a form of justice with such far-reaching consequences for the sake of upholding a system that has been causing serious damage to children for more than 30 years.

The Austrian justice system has been instructed by the politicians to deprive fathers of their custody rights, and it has been implementing the destruction of the father-child relationship without a second thought. This even applies to the rare cases where the father has sole custody – as even after the lapse of years the child's mother can put in an application, with the support of the youth welfare office, arbitrary social workers and cowardly judges, and get the situation turned around again.

With sole custody the child loses the duality of upbringing, the variety of different points of view coming from both parents, and thus also the assurance of being able to experience both parents for its own good and benefit. For a child losing one parent is like losing an eye – it becomes blind on one side.

No judge dares go against the tendencies of general case law, even if he knows very well that the judgments pronounced are unjust. It would not benefit his career if he were to give judgment in opposition to the main stream of the judicature.

This is a conscious and deliberate abuse of office.

More than 90% of all legal decisions in custody cases go against the father.

Is this coincidence, or is it deliberate and arbitrary choice on the side of social policy, imposed from the top down?

It is high time to state things clearly as they are. This is an incomprehensibly improper situation, unworthy of a sophisticated state founded on the rule of law, and it is built into the administration of what passes for justice today.

It causes acute damage to the citizens affected, because they lose their faith in democracy and the rule of law.

Parenthood is a lifelong obligation which cannot be destroyed by the laws!

If a state has the audacity to make parents into outlaws by judicial decree, it loses the entitlement to be the objective regulatory authority and to determine the social lives of the members of society. A parent should not be deprived of rights unless a reasonable case can be made that the child needs to be protected. But in the great majority of cases there is absolutely no sign of this. The mother's wish to be left in peace, her wanting to make decisions relating to the children without interference, must be seen as insufficient grounds for the father's being deprived of custody.

But this is what happens all the time.

From the legal point of view the mother is now the 'sole parent' – a situation she has herself brought about by proceeding as described earlier. The term 'mother on her own' is a magic word for all the authorities. Now she can put in applications, always casting herself in the role of victim, pocket all child benefit single-handed, demand tax credits, turn the screw on the ex by insisting on ever higher support payments, apply for rent assistance, help herself to social welfare and so on – and all this at the expense of the state.

And all this because evidently the 'mother on her own' is the being most in need of protection in our society.

The sole parent, the mother who has been given sole custody, is in possession of all the rights that Austrian family policy is able to offer in this country.

The financial benefits are obvious.

Then she has the free choice of a partner, along with the option of transferring the right of care which has been withdrawn from the biological father to this new partner, based on her own fully autonomous judgment.

Whether the children like it or not. And whether the biological father likes it or not.

The fatherless society is evidently a family policy model we are being enjoined to support.

The extreme version of this family model at the expense of this state now looks as follows. The mother, with the children, lives with state support in adequate accommodation. The new substitute father moves in, though without stating this address as his official residence, so that the mother does not lose her right of state support. Nor is the mother going to get married, because that would mean losing the right to maintenance payments from her ex.

The biological father, deprived of his rights and deprived of custody, continues to be obliged to pay maintenance for the children – and in many cases for the mother as well.

A fine state of affairs.

So as things are in practice today, based on judgments by the Austrian courts in violation of human rights and the briefs of conscienceless lawyers, mothers are encouraged to put in an application for the transfer of provisional sole custody, because this has excellent chances of being granted.

Although the formulation of the courts uses the word 'provisional', *de facto* this can be understood as entailing 'permanent' or 'final'.

Even in the wording of such judgments fathers are being lied to.

Chapter 5

Visiting rights

With custody having been withdrawn, we have come a good way towards depriving the father of his rights, and the children of the two parents are also given to understand as much, in that they hear on repeated occasions that now there will be no more disagreements because the father no longer has any say.

The father in this position hesitantly comes to accept his deprivation of rights by the Austrian Republic, based on the principle that 'joint custody is only possible in a case where both parents wish it'.

A plainer indication could not possibly be given.

The mother only has to state that she doesn't want joint custody, and right away she has reached her goal – that of putting the father on the scrap heap.

The youth welfare office will be told that the father is not a good father and that joint custody would not be beneficial to the children, and this 'authority' immediately takes up a position – doing whatever the mother wants under the pretext of child welfare, and when the desperate father raises objection they will just shrug their shoulders and point to 'the way the law stands'. But at the same time they will point out that visiting rights are still being upheld, after all, and that of course is a whole lot more important.

So the father swallows the pill in the matter of custody, and pins his hopes on visiting rights.

For fathers and their children separation almost always means a massive diminution of the father-child relationship, which before separation was usually an intensive one.

Quite apart from the fact that following separation, contact between the separated parent and the child can in any case only be seen as a residual minimum of a family life, the term 'visiting rights' is itself highly revealing of what as a rule it actually turns out to be – to be able to visit one's own children only on an application to the court, to be regarded as a 'visitor', one who must confine himself strictly to prescribed visiting hours.

Just like a former family member or like a distant relation, the father is now just entitled to have the children 'handed over' to him in a washed and brushed state, and must 'repatriate' them punctually to the mother in an equally washed and brushed state at the appointed time.

A humiliating performance every other weekend. Notwithstanding fathers put themselves through it out of love for their children, and every time leave what is now the new door of the house with unspeakable pain. Separation from one's own child is in most cases a 'threshold experience', and involves severe and long persisting traumatisation of fathers and their children.

What mother would ever accept such treatment?

How could one explain to a mother that from now on she is only entitled to visit her child every two weeks, and that the child must be brought back to the father at just the agreed time and not a minute later?

What mother would put up with it? What pain would be imposed on her in such a situation?

So why is it expected of a father? Why and by what justification do people distinguish between a mother's and a father's love?

This is where the biological processes come into play.

Since the start of women's emancipation, you see, it has always been claimed that everything is nurture rather than nature – there is no difference between men and women, they must be viewed as having equal rights!

When it is a matter of custody or visiting rights, all these decades of effort to bring about equal rights are suddenly invalidated. Now we find it asserted as a fact of nature that a mother represent the stronger emotional bond for the child.

Suddenly the mother is the being who has carried the child for nine months in the womb, who has had to undergo the pains of childbirth and who has felt an intimate affection in feeding and looking after the child. It is unthinkable that a mother's love for her child could be comparable with the love of the father who has merely engendered it. At the same time we find it expected today, quite justifiably, that fathers will be concerned with the child from the time it is born, will help look after it and care for it in every way, and in most cases this is already the reality of the situation.

So for modern fathers it is all the more incomprehensible and painful to be told on all sides, following a separation, that after all they are 'only a father'. They just cannot understand why suddenly their love is no longer wanted, and they are fobbed off with the argument that 'the children belong to the mother' – because of the biological facts.

It is a strange interpretation of equal rights and of feminism's previous stringent denial of biological predetermination.

When it comes to visiting rights, the father is simply degraded to the status of a visitor – in the form of a favourite uncle who comes twice a month and hopefully comes bearing gifts, or at least is willing to lay out the odd euro or two – in addition, of course, to his statutory maintenance obligations.

The cost of the journey and of eating out on visiting weekends, of course, are something he has to cover without any kind of assistance. After all, he is the father!

All based on the motto that he who begets the child is also able to pay!

But no, he is not a father any longer.

He gets told that he has an important function if he behaves nicely and comes to visit every fourteen days. He definitely does not have any real fatherly function, his only function is that of the visitor who pays. And this function too he has only received on loan, because if the mother changes her mind or new life circumstances are created, he can lose the last remnant of this opportunity of contact at any time.

Without any consequences for the mother, of course.

What is perhaps the worst and most humiliating form of what goes by the name of visiting rights is the 'visiting café'.

Just imagine the following situation: once a month (!) a father is allowed to see his two children for one hour (!) 'under supervision' at a place designated for the purpose by the 'Mothers' Welfare Office'. Of course at his own expense. He does want to see his children, after all!

Like a criminal on parole, the father will be put under surveillance in this situation – to see whether he behaves 'properly toward the children', and everything will be recorded and reported back to the Mothers' Welfare Office. Without the father's having any opportunity of reading the social worker's report! Of course the Mothers' Welfare Office doesn't allow you to inspect the files.

Woe betide him if the 'social worker' present decides that the father has said 'something wrong' to the children, or perhaps approached them in an impermissible way – for example, if he wants to give them a hug.

Over and above the inhuman conditions of this visiting café, this kind of meeting is going to give the children the impression that their father might somehow be 'dangerous' or 'unpredictable' – because otherwise, of course, there would be no objection to his meeting his children alone.

All this under the pretext of 'visiting supervision' or the 'supportive facilitation of contact'. In reality this scenario is created for the purpose of keeping the father under observation and letting the mother know what he has spoken to the children about. A fascist paranoid enormity of total control addiction on the part of Mothers' Welfare, acting on the instructions of the arbitrary courts.

If the father prefers not to take part in this travesty, which seems altogether very understandable, he is out of it entirely and at once – the only choice left to him is either not to see his children at all, or to accept the conditions of the Mothers' Welfare Office.

To quote the actual words that were used: 'Either you go to the visiting café or you don't see your children at all!'

Sadly there are now also mothers who are forced into this kind of supervised contact with their own child, and they report having the same experience as the fathers.

Astonishing to relate, the affected fathers often put up with this form of psychological torture for years – putting themselves through it because often it is their only chance of seeing their children, because they love their children and hope against hope that at some time in the future this humiliation will come to an end and 'normal visiting rights' will be awarded. If the father has been a good boy for months or years, has behaved properly in the visiting café and paid for it of course like a nice chap, one day Mothers' Welfare may suggest to the court that it might be worth 'giving it a try' with visits once a week or so. Extensions of 'normal visiting rights every fortnight' are generally turned down by the court. We then find it written in many expert reports that 'extended visiting rights would be detrimental to the child's welfare'. The two-weekly rhythm is a dogma that cannot be challenged, and only serves the purpose of keeping the father more at a distance.

First of all alienation is allowed to come about and legalised, and then the father has to accept this kind of 'facilitated contact' and pay for it.

What a farce!

Or is it just a job creation scheme for the employees of the Mothers' Welfare Office and the visiting café?

So fathers are expected to pay for their own deprivation of rights and alienation from the child by financing the visiting café, the Mothers' Welfare Offices, the lawyers, judges and upholders of the law – not to speak of the remorseless obligation of maintenance – often going to the point of financial annihilation?

If the father 'fails to comply' with the rulings of the authorities, for instance because he wants to see his children more often, he will live to regret it. Vengeance will not be long in coming, the Mothers' Welfare Office and the courts will descend on the 'uncooperative and incorrigible father', while the mother naturally is left untouched even when visiting rights are reduced to nothing as a result.

As an example, we may refer to a case connected with the author's support activities under the auspices of the 'Väter ohne Rechte' ['Fathers Without Rights'] association. The mother in this case had successfully boycotted the father's visiting rights – with the full knowledge of Mothers' Welfare and the court – for a whole year. The father tried all the same to have contact with his five-year-old son, but was only successful on rare occasions, because the mother did everything she could to prevent it. After a year the court issued a decree granting the father 'standard visiting rights in keeping with child welfare, every fourteen days'. Up till then the father had repeatedly tried to pay his son short visits at the child's kindergarten. The kindergarten teacher was aware of the situation, and reported about the loving relationship between the father and the little boy. But one day, in the course of his scanty visits to the kindergarten, the father was informed by the kindergarten teachers that the social worker from the Youth Welfare Office had been to see them and forbidden them to allow any contact between the child and his father – otherwise he would send the police and have the father forcibly removed. The father met the 'social worker' and requested an explanation, saying he did not yet have a written decree of the court in his hands, but it made him happy to see his son at least once a week at the kindergarten, often indeed only through the fence. The answer of the Youth Welfare official, who had done nothing whatever about the mother's boycotting visiting rights for the whole year, was shocking even to the present author: 'Well, what do you expect, you have visiting rights every fourteen days, just stick with that and everything will be OK.' In response to the question whether in his view it was going to have any bad effect on the child if the father came by the kindergarten from time to time and said Hi to his son, the social worker replied, 'That is not relevant, I just go by what the court decrees', stating that he had been obliged to take immediate action in accordance with the decree issued by the court – even though no written decree had yet been sent to the father – because this was what the child's mother wanted. So he had instructed the kindergarten not to allow the father to see his son, threatening them with police intervention. And incidentally, he did not see in this any violation or even anything disproportionate in the exercise of his official obligations and authority. Take me to court if you like – he wouldn't turn a hair, because he knew it would come to nothing.

This arrogant attitude of the 'Youth .Welfare Office' is what makes fathers desperate, and it is often the reason why fathers no longer bother to have any dealings with the authorities. This is all perfectly acceptable to the useless Youth Welfare officials, who don't want to hear anything the father has to say, because in any case he only makes trouble. They don't care an iota about the child's welfare, though nonetheless it is frequently used as an argument, e.g. in the formulation 'The father is granted visiting rights every fourteen days, additional contact would be DETRIMENTAL to the welfare of the child'. They are the real experts, the ladies and gentlemen of the Youth Welfare Office, isn't that so?

In the eyes of the authorities fathers are just troublemakers. They are free game that anyone can shoot down at any time, and the gutless vicarious agents of the justice department just have a field day taking pot shots at them.

The arbitrary power of authorities indoctrinated by feminism is the new fascism, and the torch-bearers of the movement have made it their objective to destroy fathers and so eliminate the family along with its product, the child.

It is the biggest and most sweeping crime since the Second World War – an apartheid system on an unprecedented scale.

Fathers are the 'niggers' of what passes for family law today. They aren't allowed to sit on the 'mothers only' bench; like the 'whites only' one, this bench at the district court and Youth Welfare Office is reserved for mothers.

Women's refuges, authorities with power of intervention, youth welfare offices and other institutes dedicated to the destruction of marriage receive millions of euros of public money for this apartheid system. If fathers seek assistance, support is generally denied them by Mother's Welfare and the courts.

It is high time for fathers to stick up for themselves!

How have fathers actually come to a point where, after a meeting lasting just one hour with a so-called 'psychological expert' in the course of the custody proceedings, their relationship with their own child gets assassinated?

In what kind of state are we actually living, when the number of hours we are 'allowed' to spend with our children is determined by people like this, over our heads and out of our control?

What an enormity! What a crime against the child!

Perhaps the following way of proceeding may seem preferable, in the eyes of some of the victims, to years of unsuccessful and sickening struggle to maintain their relationship with their own child. (This is an extract from a speech made by the author on 7.6.2011, at demonstration in the heart of Vienna).

WE ARE HERE TODAY BECAUSE THE JUSTICE DEPARTMENT IS ABUSING THE RIGHTS OF OUR CHILDREN!

WE REFUSE:

TO GO TO WOMEN EXPERTS IN THE KNOWLEDGE THAT THE RESULT IS A FOREGONE CONCLUSION AND WILL GO AGAINST US AND OUR CHILDREN!

WE REFUSE:

TO GO ON PUTTING UP WITH THE VIOLATION OF RIGHTS BY THE ORGANS OF JUSTICE!

WE REFUSE:

TO ACCEPT JUDGES WHO DO NOTHING!

WE REFUSE:

TO GO TO THE YOUTH WELFARE OFFICE, WHERE WE WILL NOT BE ABLE TO ACHIEVE ANYTHING FOR OURSELVES OR FOR OUR CHILDREN!

WE REFUSE:

TO CONTINUE TO PUT UP WITH THE MASSIVE VIOLATIONS OF HUMAN RIGHTS IN FAMILY LAW, COMMITTED BY JUDGES, EXPERTS AND THE DIVORCE INDUSTRY!

WE CALL FOR AN END TO ARBITRARY JUSTICE!

AND END TO THE STATE RAPE OF OUR CHILDREN!

AN END TO THE LEGALISED MURDER OF RELATIONSHIPS!

CHILDREN HAVE A RIGHT TO BOTH PARENTS, WITHOUT ANY IFS AND BUTS!!!

3705 OGH [Austrian Supreme Court of Justice]:
   Visiting rights, according to § 148, section 1 of the ABGB [Austrian General Civil Code]
   are a fundamental right of the child-parent relationship, and a human right that should generally be acknowledged, under the protection of article 8 of the European Human Rights Convention.

The sinister troika of the Youth Welfare Office, the experts they consult and the family courts are obstructing this right of the child over and over again.

Chapter 6

Alienation and PAS

If you want to be a father in this country, you need to be aware that you can only be involved in the lives of your children as long as the mother allows it!

If separation occurs, you will be catapulted out of the family and degraded to the status of a visitor under the obligation of maintenance, entitled only to brief encounters with your child, loaned out for a while but still belonging to the mother.

The difference it makes to see, feel and look after one's child on a daily basis, to be able to involve oneself in the child's development, as opposed to being suddenly reduced to seeing these small persons every two weeks, is something of which every father who has suffered from this regime is well aware.

Only the mothers don't know, because they hardly ever get into this situation!

And be it said that those fathers who are entitled to visiting rights at all are still in a relatively fortunate position.

As a result of suggestion and brainwashing, unfortunately, many children are influenced in such a way that they don't even want to have contact with the visiting father any longer. The physiological basis for this is what is known as 'neuroplasticity', namely the capability of the child's brain of forming new neurons and synapses and so adapting to new situations, in both a physical and an emotional sense.

Many mothers know that children are absolutely controllable, and instrumentalise them in this way.

This is because it is entirely in the hands of the mother to see that contact between the child and the father takes place. As a result, fathers now find themselves in a new relation of dependency on the mother, a dependency that is actually even stronger now than it was before the separation.

With many mothers it is going to depend on the way they are feeling, their mood or their current life situation whether, when and for how long the father can see his child.

Not infrequently vengeful feelings are the controlling element when it is a question whether visiting rights will be exercised, or a valid legal decision obstructed.

In an extreme case, contact between the child and the father will be just 'turned off'.

Or visiting contact will be linked to new demands in connection with maintenance payments.

Here the authorities would have an opportunity of getting involved. They should work to counter the alienation that results from the mother's obstructing the visiting arrangements.

The fatal truth, however, is that they don't do anything.

The path to the Youth Welfare Office and the courts is a stony one.

The monstrous regiment of women at Mothers' Welfare speak soft words on repeated occasions – they promise to talk to the mother and the children. Unfortunately it then emerges that the children no longer want any contact, or the mother brings new accusations against the father, so that the Youth Welfare Office is sadly no longer responsible and it is a matter to be referred to the custody court. But this wilful abdication of responsibility on the part of the youth welfare officials immediately comes to an end when a the custody court, in return, requests a position statement from the Youth Welfare Office. This will then duly inform them that, based on 'the state of the law', joint custody or visiting rights 'under compulsion' appear not to be an option.

Notwithstanding, any father who values his children and contact with his children, is going to try everything he can and tread the frustrating path of visits to the authorities. All fathers conscious of their responsibility will try all the legal resources at their disposal, and have recourse to the far too long-drawn-out rigmarole of going through the proper channels. They do this out of love for their children.

As so often described and experienced, all these efforts more often than not end up meeting with a shrug of the shoulders and the standard response, 'I'm sorry, I do understand your position, but there's nothing I can do.' The father needs to make all the running and exert himself, no one is going to level reproaches at the mother if she is uncompromising. On the contrary, we often hear it said, 'I guess the mother must have her reasons for acting this way.'

The triumph of the mother is absolute – she can punish the father by withdrawing child access whenever she wants, without the least consequence. This means she is capable of hitting him where it hurts. Some judges may just tentatively try to impose 'coercive penalties', or summon the mother in order to remind her of her obligations.

In reality this is not going to change anything, and alienation resulting from the boycott of visiting rights proceeds apace.

Every day without contact between father and child helps the mother to reach the desired result and exacerbates the alienation, whether deliberately intended by the mother or not.

Here are the shocking figures: with a divorce rate of almost 50% (in urban districts up to 60%), something like 40% of fathers and their children end up having no contact at all within one or two years from the time of separation!

The lack of contact and resulting distance then give rise to what has been called PAS (Parental Alienation Syndrome). This is the extreme variant of the abuse of the child by active or passive suggestion and brainwashing, and ends up with the child refusing to have any contact with the father at all.

On the one hand this is the result of a conflict of loyalties; on the other, it is self-protection – the children fall into an attitude of solidarity with the mother, coupled with an equally ingrained rejection of the father. Frequently they develop a conspicuously hostile attitude which embraces the father's family as well, even if they have done nothing to deserve it.

Nobody imposes any checks, and the father can only look on helplessly as the mother proceeds towards her objective.

This is an altogether painful experience, a situation that the father simply cannot make sense of. Often the shape of things is like this:

My calls are no longer answered, why?

SMS messages are no longer being answered, why?

Letters are not being answered, why?

Presents are sent back, why?

Contact is rejected, why?

We love each other after all, why is it all happening like this?

Because the neuroplasticity of the child's senses functions in favour of the mother's suggestions, and the example of emotional distance from the father that she presents transmits itself to the child's brain, thus forming a replica of whatever the mother wants.

Here is a detailed plan of action for mothers seeking to reach the goal of alienation and PAS:

Separation

The best thing is to move away, and take the children with you. This is not child abduction – though it would be if the father were responsible!

Commando-style deportation of the children you share – just remove them from the familiar environment.

Or do anything it takes to have the father subjected to a restraining order. This is a method of proven effectiveness for getting rid of him. Just call the police and make a statement to the effect that you, as a woman, feel under threat, or provoke a confrontation and state that you have suffered bodily injury. But it is even enough just to say, 'I'm scared'. As a result the police will be obliged to order the father of the family out of the joint apartment. Only a court decree will be able to lift the restraining order. It is easy to picture what chances a banished father will have in the coming divorce and custody proceedings, even if it should turn out that he is innocent. In cases where a restraining order has been imposed without justification, an action for defamation is objectively not going to stand a chance.

It all goes through without any legal consequences for the mother.

Maintenance

Demand maintenance immediately! As a result of the separated household, the father (whether or not he is responsible for the separation) is obliged to provide maintenance, thus depriving him right from the start of any equality of opportunity in connection with the future financial burdens resulting from the divorce. If the father refuses to pay, an order of compulsory enforcement will be issued immediately.

It all goes through without any ifs or buts.

Apply for sole custody

As a result of the new situation the father is powerless and paralysed, and the application often comes as a surprise. The argument offered in support is the new self-created situation of child care, and the first underhand moves against the father come into play.

It's always the same arguments. The children are afraid of their father. The father is violent. The father is suspected of paedophile tendencies. The children have been neglected by the father. The father is incapable of looking after the children properly. He is unreliable, he is late bringing the children back. He drinks, he has unsuitable friends, impossible new life partners...

Motto: there's bound to be something in it, a woman wouldn't say things like that if there weren't any reason for it, surely?

So it all goes through, without the truth of the matter being checked in any way.

Visiting arrangements

Just sign anything you have to, *pro forma*! That way you give the impression that you are willing to compromise. I am a good mother, you say, because you are in favour of visiting rights.

Don't feel bound by it, influence the children's minds, and then you can always argue that the children don't want to see their father. Put the main emphasis on 'what the children want'.

That goes through as well – the mother has no consequences to fear.

Just a note on 'what the children want': it is obvious and has been sufficiently proved by psychological experts that what children want does not necessarily coincide with the best thing for the children's welfare.

For example, if what the children want is expressed in their saying 'I don't want to go to school', this will on the whole be ignored, because it is plain that attending school is beneficial for the child, and so the child will be persuaded, and if necessary even coerced into going to school.

With visiting rights, it is the other way around.

Boycott visiting rights

Use commonplace arguments – the children have got something planned, a birthday party or something, they can't make it this weekend, they have some special occasion, they are ill, they are allergic to the father's dog or cat, the father is mean to them, the father says bad things about the mother, we are off on a short break, the father neglects them, he has a bad relationship with them or he suffers from a psychological condition.

All these are weapons which can issue in the sacrosanct slogan, 'threat to the children's welfare'.

First of all, the mother will have recourse to the so-called 'good behaviour clause'. The father has said bad things about the mother – and that, of course, is strictly forbidden!

This code of behaviour, oddly enough, only applies to the father – who checks or scrutinises what the mother says about the father, in the child's presence?

Again it is the children who report to the mother about what the father says and the way he behaves – like well trained child soldiers, they must render account for the time they have spent with their father. Again they are instrumentalised and trained in the mother's surveillance system, as a result of which she will then be able to put in a report to the Youth Welfare Office.

At Youth Welfare all the alarm bells ring. Even if it is not Youth Welfare's responsibility.

But now it is.

Often fathers swallow the refusal of visiting rights without protest, in the hope that perhaps next time there won't be a problem. Compensation for the missed hours or days of contact is rarely going to be provided.

Indeed, we even find cases where notice is given of the violation of the father's rights. For example, the father is notified in writing that his recognised visiting rights have been suspended in view of a subsequent engagement in connection with an expert report. The reasons for this deliberate obstruction of contact between father and child is the putative 'influence on the child's statements to the psychological expert as a result of visiting contact with the father'. The children might say, of course, that their visit to their father last weekend was quite OK. Such utterances might even give the expert assessor cause to extend visiting rights. But this is clearly undesirable, so when an expert report is anticipated, we often find that contact is broken off abruptly and altogether.

The Youth Welfare Office and the court look on and do nothing.

And all that goes through, without any consequences for the mother.

Legalise the process of alienation

Apply for suspension of visiting rights! For the arguments, see the above.

Always argue that 'The children don't want to visit, there's nothing I can do!'

That too will be accepted – with the blessing of an expert report, and acquiring legal effect on the basis of a court decree. The courts will dance to the mother's tune.

Psychological expert reports

The father goes to the responsible court and informs them about the lack of visiting contact. The judge says, 'Oh dear, I'm afraid we need an expert report from a specialist, because – even with 25 years of experience as a judge in family law – I do not myself feel capable of making a decision.'

The father is optimistic that the psychological expert will realise what is going on.

Again he is way off the mark. The expert report comes down entirely on the side of the mother, with a recommendation of suspension of visiting rights, or allowing visiting only under supervision, in the form of a visiting café. The judge says, 'Thank God I was not responsible for this recommendation, but the psychological experts, after all, must know what they are doing!' And he is happy to approve the report, without taking any counter-arguments into consideration, because he can then at last consider the case closed.

The father's lawyer advises against making any appeal, because 'there would be no point'; again, it is a matter of 'the way the law stands'. Or better still, it's the father's fault, because he hasn't come up with the required 'good behaviour'.

Something with which the mother is never charged.

An example

In the strength of a court decree, the children's father is refused custody and has visiting rights provisionally suspended. When the divorce becomes legally effective, the tentative recommendation is made that the father be allowed to visit the two children under supervision, once a month and for just one hour (extract from the decree of the Federal Court of Krems of 9.12.2008, file reference 17P 241/07f, in the guardianship proceedings of the present writer).

As a result the mother has actually achieved her goal in juridical terms, and the father and his children are separated for years.

This is not an isolated case. It happens repeatedly and is enforced by court decrees, a decision that leaves the father speechless.

In this connection it is important to state clearly that not all mothers make a practice of child abduction along these lines. I would like to express my thanks at this point to the many responsible mothers who tell their children that in spite of separation the father is still a parent, and remains important for the child's further development.

These are the ones who truly have the child's welfare at heart, rather than inflicting on the children the consequence of their obsessive attitudes and personal resentment of the father.

Those mothers, on the other hand, who have made it their goal to deprive the father and the children of all rights find it an extremely easy game to abuse their position as 'sole parent' shamelessly. With the help of 'the present state of the law', and having all economic advantages on their side, they are well capable of 'killing off' the father, and they can do it without ever being held to account.

But there are also approaches for the legal implementation of academic findings on the matter of parent-child alienation, or PAS as it is also known.

On 26.8.2010 the Republic of Brazil passed a law defining 'parental alienation' as a crime subject to legal penalties, as a form of child abuse (Statute 12 318, as a modification of Article 236 of Statute 8069 13). This law gives judges the option of introducing effective measures to combat cases of parental alienation. These can include financial penalties, and there may also be consequences for custody rights or in relation to decisions on residence or supervision issues.

At this point we may also refer to what is known as the Cochem Model, according to which the parent responsible for the alienation will be threatened with the loss of custody. The success rate of this system is around 90%! In Austria this would be unthinkable, because the old argument that penalising the mother would be detrimental to the child's welfare evidently continues to hold good. The success of Judge Jürgen Rudolph, applying the Cochem system, demonstrates that the mere threat is sufficiently effective and can result in many cases in preventing the loss of contact between father and child.

Dr Richard Gardner gives an even clearer account of the possibilities of obviating PAS. Out of 99 cases of PAS investigated, in 22 cases the recommendation that custody be transferred to the alienated parent (though always involving strict requirements that contact be kept up with the parent who had enjoyed custody before) was adopted by the court. In all cases without exception where custody was transferred, PAS disappeared without trace. In the cases where the court went against the recommendations of the expert consulted and left custody with the parent responsible for the alienation, PAS continued to be clearly detectable, based on a scrutiny following an interval of several years, or indeed to be even more marked than before (see R. Gardner: Das elterliche Entfremdungs-Syndrom, Anregungen zur Intervention durch begleitende Berufe [Parental Alienation Syndrome – Recommendations for Intervention by the Support Professions], VWB, Berlin, 2002).

In Austria, however, the reality of the law looks quite different. The district courts and the Youth Welfare Office are arbitrary agents of the mother's omnipotence, and act to legalise the alienation of fathers from their children.

Child robbery and the destruction of the family are regarded as socially respectable. The image that comes to mind is of the shoulder-shrugging judge – Kafkaesque, but altogether real in this case.

Family judges behave like nursery school children: I can't help it, there's nothing I can do about it, the expert report states as follows, what am I to do, I have to abide by the legal requirements, and so on and so forth. A pathetic picture of the representatives of our justice system, who so like to present themselves to the outside world as 'strong and independent judges'.

We often come across the argument that children must be protected from the supposedly violent father. With equal frequency, this assertion fails to stand up to closer examination.

But no decree of an Austrian district court, and no report from the Mothers' Welfare Office will be found to contain the statement that 'Children must be protected against the loss of a parent!'

The only chance of improving the PAS symptoms affecting the children or overcoming them altogether (at all events where PAS is moderately severe to severe) is by transferring custody to the alienated parent and restricting contact with the parent responsible for the alienation. In Austria, however, such action is practically unthinkable, because the judges are too ignorant and cowardly to take such a courageous step in the children's best interests.

PAS children moreover need a suitable PAS therapist, one who is specially trained in diagnosis and familiar with the necessary therapeutic measures. With the majority of the experts in the field of psychology who work for the courts on the oath, as well as many psychotherapists in private practice, this is not going to be the case. This is the reason why hundreds of thousands of children suffering from PAS never receive therapy. As a result of ignorance and stupidity, they remain the victims of the alienating parent who has programmed the condition in the first place. The consequences for our children are sufficiently well known, but are deliberately denied by the authorities or else totally ignored.

We frequently find the argument based on 'parental conflict' advanced as a reason why contact between father and child should be restricted.

PAS is NOT a case of parental conflict. It is active child abuse, with serious consequences for the child. This too is something the Austrian justice system is aware of, but it is not to be found in any of the decrees pronounced by family judges.

Chapter 7

Maintenance

Now the father has been reduced to the status of a *Zahlvater* – a cash cow, a mere source of income.

What does this mean? It is practically the terminal state for a good many years, years during which the father will repeatedly be faced with the tormenting question – Why do I have to pay for children who have been taken away from me? Anyone will understand that a financial contribution to the welfare of 'one's own' children does need to be made – but what if these children are out of reach, in the sense that no adequate contact remains, not even a minimal but nonetheless visible contact between father and child?

With our 'legal system', the mere fact of biological descent is sufficient grounds for a claim to maintenance – even when the parent has no contact with the child whatsoever.

This ruling contradicts every sense of justice and only serves to assure the mother of an additional 'income' – in addition, be it noted, to the 'child benefit' to which she is entitled. This is a transfer of capital with far-reaching consequences.

And it generally gives rise to a skewed position in financial terms: the father has to pay, and the mother pockets the proceeds. This state of affairs is clearly motivated by social policy. It reinforces the rights of the mother (cleverly dressed up, for the sake of argument, as the rights of the children) and places them above the fundamental principle of equality.

This is an area where the state needs to meet its responsibilities. Rights and obligations should be linked, in such a way that the amount of maintenance payments bears a graduated relation to the frequency of contact with the child.

No doubt we would suddenly find many children visiting their fathers at weekends not even included in the agreed visiting arrangements. No prizes for guessing why.

But the very opposite is in practice the case.

No one is concerned whether contact between father and child is kept up.

Maintenance payments are completely detached from visiting rights.

Let me just mention at this point that the Family Law Reform of 2009 represented another decisive step in the direction of the 'fatherless society'.

So-called 'patchwork families' were to be put on an equal footing, in legal terms, with a 'proper family'. Of course, in formulating the legal principles for this objective, no one thought to ask the opinion of the fathers who would be affected by the change.

The only contributions to implementation of the new legislation came from 'affected mothers' and 'family policy experts'.

It is not hard to see what the matter amounts to, and what social form of the family is recommended to us as the shape of the future.

The mother will determine, at every moment in time from the birth of the child on, who is to be the 'father' or entitled to be recognised as such. The life partner of the mother (even if he is not the biological father of her children) can have 'rights of custody', if the mother desires it, in respect of the child to whom he is not related. The biological father can be traded in at any point against a new partner whom the mother finds preferable, who will inherit the rights of the physical father.

The physical father, though, is going to be left with obligations, and nothing else – the obligation to provide maintenance.

Obligations, but no rights – seeing that these have been transferred to the 'new father'.

The latter, meanwhile, can only continue to be a 'substitute father' so long as he enjoys the favour of the mother. If the mother changes her mind, the substitute father will be replaced by the next one.

Where are the children in all this, where is child welfare?

Nobody puts this question in connection with these issues.

Here again we see 'mother's rights' being set above the rights of the children and the rights of the physical father.

Many men will think long and hard before starting a family, when they know what can happen, and in fact frequently does occur in practice.

This forces us inevitably to contemplate the question of social development in Austria. Childless marriages are on the increase, as is the reluctance of many young people to get married.

Demographic developments show clearly that the pension system in its present form can only be maintained on the basis of increased immigration.

Is this the declared aim of Austrian family policy?

The many 'single mothers' must receive support from the state – altogether amounting to a large proportion of social benefits overall.

Is this too the declared aim of Austrian family policy?

At the same time many fathers obliged to pay maintenance are compelled to work on the black market, just to keep their heads above water financially.

This causes massive damage to the Austrian state, in view of the evaded tax payments.

Again, is this the declared aim of Austrian family policy?

No, it can't be the aim of Austrian family policy – but it certainly is a declared aim of 'women's policy', so-called, which receives, generates and forces through indefensibly high subsidies as a result of the 'legitimate concerns of feminist politics' being upheld by the parties in parliament capable of forming a majority.

The state has abdicated from its responsibilities, and lets the fathers pay – rather than itself helping him out with the costs that have been incurred through the destruction of the family.

'Maintenance advance' it is called, this form of prepayment – whereby millions of euros are advanced by the state every year and transferred to the self-appointed sole parent. Naturally this money has to be reclaimed, under threat of compulsory enforcement, from the father, even if this brings him close to financial ruin. 'Child welfare' again serves as the pretext for this – the abusive argument so frequently used to justify the state's proceedings against the father.

At the expense of the state and of fathers deprived of custody – under the pretext of 'equal rights' and with lasting consequences for the children as future shapers of society – an egotistical social model subordinated to the war of the sexes is being financed.

Women's frequently cited 'financial independence from the man' immediately comes to an end when it is a question of ripping off the father. Now the father is shamelessly called on to function as a cash cow, while the feminist objective of women's independence is promptly invalidated. Forty percent of divorced women would have no income if it were not for maintenance payments from their ex.

Austrian justice is aware of this, and yet does nothing about this unjust situation in family law, because politically its hands are tied.

Any justice minister who tried to redress this injustice and reverse the massive discrimination against fathers in Austrian family law would be shot to pieces, and would very soon be obliged to resign from office. This as a result of pressure from the 'single mothers' who enjoy the fruits of the present unjust situation and have strong political representation, even though this group only accounts for 13.2% (in absolute figures, around 100,000 single mothers) of families with children under the age of 25.

What is at stake here is the flow of funds and nothing else!

The rising number of persons constituting this electoral group is seen as desirable. It is encouraged, because this will ensure the political survival of the feminists.

At the children's expense, a fatherless society is being created.

It is sufficiently well known that fatherless children and young people show an increased risk of aggression, youth criminality, drug dependence, relationship problems (with early but unstable partnerships) and significantly higher separation and divorce rates. This is how the traumatisation perpetuates itself into the next generation.

The future will reveal whether emotionally crippled, fatherless children are capable of directing the affairs of the state in such a way that justice and equal rights for all citizens in our country can be preserved.

Chapter 8

Waiting

It is like an incurable chronic disease, or like contracting cancer with an uncertain outcome – waiting for one's children.

Waiting for an answer to so many letters.

Waiting for an answer to countless calls and SMS messages.

Waiting for the decision of the court.

Waiting for the long-desired contact with your own child.

Waiting for the children to grow up soon – perhaps after all they will get in touch one day in order to find out what their father is doing, what his version of the separation sounds like.

Every day you are thinking about your child, who you haven't seen for years now, but who did after all live for all of ten years with both parents.

How is it possible that my children do not want to see me – after all, I have always had a loving relationship with these small beings who need protection and who struggle for their share of love, and I have actually told them that they will always be able to count on me.

Using the words, 'I love you and I will always be there for you,' you have tried to give the children security and make it clear to them that you are never going to abandon them. In spite of this, contact has come to a stop.

Because my children have been removed from me by their mother.

Because the mother is now vested in all the relevant rights, and does not want me to have any contact with the children.

Because the children's mother has deliberately avoided ever uttering the most important sentence for children of separated families, 'We have separated, but he will still always be your father, and I want it to be possible for you to continue to meet him on a regular basis.'

No child hearing this sentence is going to reject the father – because children love both parents, and do not want to lose either of them.

They suffer a conflict of identity, which of course needs to be overcome.

But not by transferring sole custody to the mother and giving her total latitude to control visiting contact at her own discretion, but rather by making sure that contact is still kept up!

In the case of acrimonious divorces, this should be the first priority of the custody court.

Visiting rights must not be tied to deadlines for establishing the legal effectiveness of the divorce (a matter which may take years).

Right at the start of the separation, immediate steps must be taken to ensure that continuous contact be maintained – if necessary, even by means of coercive penalties and the threat of loss of custody.

This should apply both to mothers who prevent contact and to fathers who fail to comply with visiting arrangements alike.

No child and no parent should be condemned to having to wait so long!

The prolonged negotiations of a contested custody case block the continuity of contact (more often than not between father and child), and the end is really going to be the father's being stripped of his rights, coupled with the rapid onset of alienation.

Children think and experience things on a much shorter time scale than adults, and for that reason decisions should be speedy!

It is completely absurd to allow the report of a psychological expert to be delayed for months, and then submit the report to the court – as in the case of the present writer – more than a year after the separation and loss of contact with the children. Not to mention presenting the alienation that has already been brought about as 'reluctance on the part of their children to see their father', and actually enshrining this in the court decree. Even if higher courts may, on occasion, recognise years later that the court of the first instance made an incorrect decision, it is much too late for normal contact to be maintained. Restoration of a healthy relationship is then often extremely difficult, or even impossible for many years.

The hierarchy of the father-child relationship in family law is as follows:

Joint custody – visiting rights – right to information.

If the highest link in the chain (joint custody) can lead to withdrawal of custody from a parent, just on the submission of an application without justification, it goes without saying that all subsequent links will be equally subject to arbitrary violation.

So why not uphold the supreme element of the hierarchy as the guarantee of the relationship in question? Answer – because the withdrawal of custody paves the way for wilful and arbitrary action! That is the real reason why joint custody is rejected by the feminists – because the feminists (as the name suggests) are in reality concerned about 'women's rights', feminist goals and financial aspects (the flow of funds), and not with children's rights or child welfare. Otherwise it is inexplicable why joint custody should be so universally opposed.

Consequently, Austrian family law as it applies today should be speedily and promptly amended, with the following changes being made:

1. Joint custody should be standard, the supplementary qualification 'Only when both parents desire it' must be completely cancelled. Both parents have 'the obligation and the right' to be concerned about the welfare of the child! The routine withdrawal of custody from one parents brings about an exacerbation of the conflict, and makes it more difficult to arrive at a compromise in the child's best interests.

2. The proceedings should be shortened to a maximum of 3 months. Only in this way can the loss of contact and resulting alienation be effectively prevented.
3. There must be a guarantee that court decrees with the force of law will actually be enforced. The recommended instruments for this would be the sensitive application of coercive penalties to the parent obstructing visiting rights, or in case of repeated nullification of visiting rights, the withdrawal of custody.
4. Dilatory judges must be reminded of their responsibilities. It is not just a matter of an insurance dispute – in this case we are concerned with the elementary right to family life and the vital interest of the child.

In the case of contested custody proceedings, all these demands depend on DE-ESCALATION (and this too is a long-established psychological fact). Likewise, the implementation of these demands would mean a massive reduction in the number and duration of proceedings.

Chapter 9

Legal aspects

The current administration of the law in the Austrian family law field violates several higher laws at once. These are as follows:

The Austrian constitution

Allgemeines bürgerliches Recht (ABGB) [the Austrian General Civil Code]

The UN Convention on Children's Rights

The European Human Rights Convention

Council of Europe, European Treaty Series ETS 192, 'Convention Concerning Contact with Children', final version between Germany, Austria and Switzerland, Strasbourg, 15.5.2003.

Explanatory notes

I) Federal Constitution of the Republic of Austria

Article 7

(1) All federal citizens are equal in the eyes of the law. Priority rights based on birth, sex, status, class or confession are hereby excluded. No one may be disadvantaged because of a handicap. The Republic (consisting of the federation, the federal states and the municipalities) is committed to ensuring equal treatment for handicapped and non-handicapped persons in all areas of daily life.

(2) The federation, the federal states and the municipalities are committed to the effective equal treatment of men and women. Measures to encourage the *de facto* equality of women and men,

especially through the removal of actually existing inequalities, are permissible.

Article 82
(1) All jurisdiction issues from the federation.
(2) Judgments and conclusions are pronounced and made out in the name of the Republic.

Elucidation

In Article 7, section (1), the equality of all citizens before the law stands in first place; in section (2) Austria expresses its commitment to the equality of man and woman. Both fundamental principles are violated in the standard administration of justice in family law.

In Article 82, section (2), it is stated that all judgments (including those in the field of family law) are promulgated in the name of the Republic. Thus it represents a legal violation of the constitution if violations of Article 7 are pronounced in the Name of the Republic.

2.) ABGB Allgemeines bürgerliches Recht (ABGB) [the Austrian General Civil Code]

§148
(1) If a parent does not live in the shared household with the child who is not yet of age, the child and this parent have the right to spend time together.

§166
The mother has sole custody in the case of children born out of wedlock. In other respects, so far as nothing has been determined

to the contrary, the stipulations relating to maintenance and custody shall apply to legitimate and illegitimate children alike.

§177

(1) If the marriage of the parents of a minor child born in wedlock is dissolved, cancelled or declared to be invalid, the custody of both parents shall not be affected. They may however submit to the court – even by way of modification of an existing regulation – an agreement for custody arrangements. The agreement may involve custody being vested either in one sole parent or in both parents. In case both parents have custody, the custody of one parent may be restricted to certain areas.

(2) In every case where both parents have custody, they must submit to the court an agreement on the question with which parent the child shall generally reside. This parent must always be the one with overall custody.

(3) The court shall be obliged to approve the parents' agreement when it is in keeping with the welfare of the child.

§177a

If, within an appropriate period from the time of the marriage of the parents being dissolved, cancelled or declared invalid, no agreement as described in § 177 above touching the principal residence of the child or the custody arrangements has been arrived at, or if the agreement is not in keeping with the welfare of the child, the court shall be obliged – if an amicable agreement cannot be reached – to decide which parent shall be given sole custody for the future.

If after the marriage has been dissolved, cancelled or declared invalid both parents have custody, as described in § 177 above, and one parent applies for the cancellation of the present custody arrangements, the court shall be obliged – if it is not possible to bring about an amicable resolution – to decide on the award of sole custody to one parent alone, having the welfare of the child at heart.

§177b

The above stipulations shall also be applicable if the parents of a minor child born in wedlock are living apart for a more than temporary period. But the court shall decide on custody, in such a case, only following an application by one of the parents.

Elucidation

§148 determines the right to personal contact between the child and the separated parent.

Obstructing this right without serious grounds based on recommendations of the Youth Welfare Office or the court represents a severe violation of a fundamental personal right, but it occurs on a regular basis, often with the support of threadbare arguments.

§166 states that from the time of the birth of a child they have engendered, unmarried fathers have no custody, that is to say no rights. This is irrespective of the question whether the father is living in the joint household, even if he is on parental leave. If he nonetheless lays claims to rights, e.g. in looking after the child or representing the child's rights in hospital, he is actually in breach of the law. In the light of the law he is NOT ALLOWED to look after the child. Thousands of unmarried fathers are living with their children and have no idea that they are actually bereft of rights. They are dependent on the goodwill of the child's mother, who can bring the partnership to an end at any time – in which case the father and his child will have no mutual rights whatever. Only with the consent of the child's mother, and following an application to the court, can an agreement for joint child care be arrived at.

At the same time, identical stipulations on maintenance apply to unmarried as to married fathers. A showcase example of 'equal rights' understood in a feminist sense.

§177 stipulates joint custody even in case of separation, subject to the proviso of mutual agreement – i.e. cases that are not contested: an amicably agreed divorce, with both parents agreeing on joint custody. An ideal case scenario, as you might say.

§177a is the classic example of a contested divorce. Here it is up to the court to bring about an agreement, which in many cases proves impossible. And this is just where, once again, the inequality of the contesting parties makes itself felt. In over 90 percent of court decisions, sole custody is awarded to the mother – and that frequently without any effective scrutiny of the child's welfare. This is associated with the resulting loss of contact between the separated parent and the child, as occurs in practically 40 percent of cases. A solution can only be found if joint custody continues in force even in this case, as there will then be very much less risk of loss of contact. This is at all events better for the child's welfare than loss of contact and increasing alienation. Sad to say, in Austria swift and superficial decisions against the child's welfare are the rule, admittedly often in a surreptitiously tendentious manner, frequently too with the blessing of a 'gender-based expert report' following the principle that 'children belong with their mothers'. A breach of law which only superficially makes it easier for the court to terminate the proceedings – at the expense of the child, one parent is deprived of rights and the child is denied its right to the parent. With one parent deprived of custody, that parent is FORBIDDEN – in the name of the Republic of Austria – to have anything to do with care of the child!

3.) UN Convention on Children's Rights

On 20 November 1989 the United Nations passed a Convention on Children's Rights. This international agreement consists of 54 articles detailing the fundamental political, social, economic, cultural and civic rights to which every child is entitled, and has already been signed and ratified by 192 states worldwide.

Austria signed the convention at the first opportunity, on 26 January 1990. On 26 June 1992 it was approved by the National Council, and on 6 August 1992 Austria filed the ratification document with the UN, so formally ratifying the Children's Rights Convention (as publicly announced in the Bundesgesetzblatt [Federal Law Gazette] 1993/7). On 5 September 1992 (30 days after the filing of the document), it formally went into effect in Austria, though with a 'reservation in respect of fulfilment' (!).

We will give a short summary here of the parts of the convention that have crucial relevance in terms of family law.

Article 5 – Respecting parental rights

The contracting states commit themselves to respecting the responsibilities, rights and obligations of the parents – or where appropriate, depending on local customs, of the members of the extended family or community, of the guardian or other persons legally responsible for the child – to direct and guide the child in the exercise of the rights assigned to the child by this agreement in a way appropriate to the child's development.

Article 8 - Identity

(1) The contracting states hereby undertake to respect the right of the child to preserve its identity, including its nationality, its name and its family relationships acknowledged under the laws and the statutes, without suffering any intervention in breach of its rights.

(2) If, in breach of the child's rights, the child is deprived of some or all components of its identity, the contracting states undertake to provide the child with every appropriate measure of assistance and protection with the aim of restoring its identity as quickly as possible.

Article 9 – Separation from the parents; personal contact

(1)   The contracting states shall ensure that a child shall not be separated from its parents against the parents' will, unless in cases where the responsible authorities, based on a decision subject to scrutiny by the courts and in accordance with the applicable legal regulations and proceedings, have determined that this separation is necessary in the interest of the child. A decision of this nature may be necessary in the individual case, if for example the child is being maltreated or abused by the parents, or if the parents are living apart and a decision needs to be taken regarding the child's place of residence.

(2) In proceedings as detailed in section 1 above, all the parties concerned shall be given the opportunity of taking part in the proceedings and expressing their opinion.

(3) The contracting states hereby commit themselves to respecting the right of the child living apart from one or both parents to maintain regular personal relations and direct contact with both parents, provided that this does not conflict with the welfare of the child.

(4) If the separation is the consequence of an action on the part of a contracting state, involving for instance detention, imprisonment, expulsion or deportation, or the death of one or both of the parents or of the child (including a death that occurs for whatever reason while the person concerned was in state custody), the contracting state hereby commits itself to supplying on request to the parents, the child or to another family member the essential information about the whereabouts of the absent family member or members, provided this shall not be detrimental to the child's welfare. The contracting states shall further ensure that the mere submission of an application of this nature shall not entail negative consequences for the person or persons in question.

Elucidation

Although the UN Convention has not been adopted in its entirety as part of the constitution, and the 'reservation in respect of fulfilment' rules out the direct application of the terms of the convention by the courts or the authorities, all the laws and statutes must conform to the convention. This is already guaranteed by the fundamental principle whereby Austrian legal prescriptions are to be interpreted in accordance with the law of nations, as well as by the country's obligation of accountability in relation to the UN Child Rights Committee.

The reservation in respect of fulfilment referred to above, which entails that the courts and authorities are not obliged to apply the terms of the convention, constitutes the juridical loophole for Youth Welfare Offices and custody courts – that is to say, these authorities can continue to act in breach of the law without being challenged under the Convention, with the consequences already familiar to us (withdrawal of custody from the father, the obligation of maintenance being retained, economic benefits to the mother and damage to the children as a result of loss of contact with the father).

4.) European Human Rights Convention

Article 8 – Right to private life and family life being respected
(1) Every person is entitled to have his or her private life and family life respected. The same applies to his or her place of residence and private correspondence.

(2) Intervention of the public authorities in such a way as to impair the exercise of this right is only legal to the extent that this intervention is provided for by law and represents a measure that is necessary in a democratic society in the interest of national security, public order and decorum, the economic welfare of the

country, the defence of order and prevention of criminal activities, or for the protection of the rights and freedoms of other persons.

Elucidation

This article states clearly that the right to family life is a fundamental human right. In Austria, however, this elementary right is being trodden underfoot – just through the frequency with which contact between parent and child is broken off, based on abuse of this fundamental human right. Every father who following separation is prevented from keeping up contact with his child is suffering injustice as a result of the decisions of the Austrian family courts. And what terrible suffering too is being inflicted on the children's emotions! This is a deliberate injury affecting at least two thirds of the family members, as a result of the will of the mother being consistently upheld – deliberately and dishonestly sold with the spin that it is in the best interests of the child.

5.) Council of Europe Treaty Series ETS 192

On 15.5.2003 the final version of the 'Übereinkommen über den Umgang von und mit Kindern' ['Convention Concerning Contact with Children'] was signed in Strasbourg by Germany, Austria and Switzerland (see http\\ conventions.coe.int./Treaty/ GER/Treaties/html/192.htm).

Articles 1-27 of this convention assert the right of the child to both parents, as well as the rights of the separated parent, and also lay the signatory countries under the obligation to implement the fundamental legal principles concerned in practice.

AUSTRIA'S SYSTEM OF JUSTICE IS IN VIOLATION OF ALL THE FUNDAMENTAL LEGAL PRINCIPLES AND CONVENTIONS LISTED ABOVE!

This is well known throughout Europe, and it is also the reason why Austria has been chosen increasingly in recent years as the ideal place of residence for mothers who wish to rid themselves of the child's father.

The Republic of Austria is widely regarded as a secret asylum and place of refuge for child abduction by alienating mothers. Even if they are subject to different regulations in their own country (e.g. joint rights of custody, or sole custody of the father), in our country everything is done to comply with the mother's wishes, with the Austrian district courts acting in breach of regulations that apply to the rest of Europe.

Chapter 10

Visions

For many years the destruction of families was associated with war, sickness, the imperative need to emigrate or criminality.

Today it is feminism, the divorce industry (with its turnover in the billions) and a completely antiquated and ignorant legal system out of line with today's academic standards, which systematically deprives parents, in most cases the father, of parental rights by mass-production methods.

Our 'modern law-based state' is the first and only form of society in the history of humanity where parenthood is denied recognition – by the state, irrevocably and in many cases without the least plausible grounds – just by the simple method of applying to a district court!

The denial of parental rights to a parent is a crime committed by the state, which is carried out as a matter of routine without any consideration of the individual circumstances, and for the most part without any relevant grounds being given.

This is in breach of all the principles of human rights.

The Republic of Austria will have to answer to the international courts of justice for this breach of law, which is being committed by Austrian district courts on a daily basis in connection with questions of custody and visiting rights.

Parenthood is for life, and must not be denied!

In custody disputes, joint custody should be seen as the standard practice!

We must do away with psychological experts who recommend, without good grounds, that a parent be deprived of custody or have visiting rights suspended, or for reasons of self-protection advise that visiting rights be exercised only under supervision!

Expert reports must be subject to scrutiny, and it must be possible to contest them effectively, when required.

A parent who tries to take away the children they share from the other parent must be made to feel the consequences!

The parent who takes the children away from the other parent notwithstanding must be made to surrender custody, because this way of behaving itself represents a risk to the child's welfare.

Inactive and dilatory family law judges must be held to account! The same applies to inactive public prosecutors who protect the dilatory judges.

As for the Youth Welfare Offices, people should have a documented right to inspection of the files!

The term 'child welfare', which forms the basis for all decisions and is so frequently misapplied, resulting in tendentious court judgments, is nowhere adequately defined in the formulations of case law.

In the author's view, the following definition of child welfare would be suitable as a basis:

1. Bodily and emotional wellbeing, as understood by the WHO definition of the term 'health'
2. The right to family life
3. The right to contact with both physical parents and their family members
4. The right to free decision and self-definition
5. The right to the maintenance of relationships with the family members of both parents after the parents have separated or divorced
6. The right to joint upbringing by both parents, as far as possible in equal proportions
7. All the rights asserted in the UN Convention on Children's Rights

8. All the rights asserted in the European Human Rights Convention
9. Protection against physical and psychological violence
10. Protection against Parental Alienation Syndrome.

Please note that the order of points from 1 to 10 is *not* a list of priorities – all these points should be seen as being of absolutely equal value.

If these points were to be taken as a reference on which court decisions were based, reality would be entirely different. Above all, it would be possible for many father-child relationships to be saved.

But the reality is in fact a violent withholding of crucial input essential to the life of the child, all this at the behest of the state, taking the form of the *de facto* legal violation of all the points given in the above definition of child welfare.

But if you try, as the present author has done, along with other people who are concerned with child welfare, to present these very concerns to the leading 'family law experts' at the Austrian Federal Ministry of Justice, with the urgent request that they work to bring about a speedy amelioration of the situation, you will find yourself confronted with the question, 'Just what kind of thing are you proposing?' and 'Please don't give us isolated sob stories!'

You could hardly find a better demonstration of the ignorance and incompetence of the civil servants who occupy such a responsible position.

The chance of changes in favour of improved children's rights is practically zero, while people like this sit in office as guardians of the law-based state, just waiting for the time when they can retire on a government pension.

The 'isolated sob story' theory is the tried and tested diversionary tactic for the cover-up of the systematic legalised withdrawal of child contact, based on court judgments in breach of justice.

Something like 100,000 Austrian fathers are prevented from seeing their children. If we include relatives on the father's side, that gives us around 600,000 victims of the system. The pretence that we have to do with just isolated cases falls down on these statistics – not to mention that practically anybody you talk to can point to a similar case occurring either in his immediate acquaintance or in his own family.

The facts of this legalised injustice must be made public. It is the duty of all citizens to make people aware of this deplorable situation at every opportunity!

Otherwise our children and young people will show even less respect for the state in future, and even less willingness to compromise on questions of social development, than they do in any case. They will have a vivid example in their mothers of the way in which you can show total lack of respect for your own father or for the government authorities, without any fear of the consequences.

More than 82% of the population is dissatisfied with Austrian justice. In many cases this is the result of the family law situation. That alone should be sufficient reason for finally bringing law and justice into closer consonance.

Poem addressed to the child's mother

In the mirror of the subconscious...

HE
He was good enough to chase after me
He was good enough to satisfy my needs
He was good enough to marry me
He was good enough to give me children
He was good enough to build a house with me
He was good enough to provide an adequate income
He was good enough to wipe up the children's messes
He was good enough to comfort the children when I was out
He was good enough to look after the children for ten years
He was good enough but I've had enough of him now
He is good enough now to be made to live without children
He is good enough now to make maintenance payments
But he is not good enough to be called a father in future
I won't allow it
I will prevent it
With all the resources at my disposal
And I will win
Because I am the mother!
HE is nobody any longer
HE – who is he?

Poem addressed to my children

The bus

On 20.8.2007 you got onto a bus, to go off on a long journey.

To begin with the bus wasn't going too fast, so that I could see your faces behind the glass and see you waving to me.

I was able to follow the bus, and at the first stops on the long trip I could see you, and you even got out briefly to spend time with me.

Then the bus went on, but I couldn't keep up with it any more. It went too fast, and it didn't make any more stops.

It drove past all the stops, and although I tried to keep up, I couldn't see your faces any longer.

But then I couldn't see the bus any more either, and you too were out of reach.

For I long time I thought I might still be able to make out the bus on the horizon – but I was wrong.

Since 5.1.2008 there haven't been any more buses, and I don't know when the next one is going to come.

But I am waiting for the bus every day, because I want to get in and go with you, to be with you on the next trip. And you know who the bus driver is. It's your mother.

Parable

To finish, here is a parable – which aims to show the reader the effects that these judicial proceedings have on human emotions.

A man (a judge, perhaps) goes to the doctor complaining of pains in the region of the heart.

The doctor says, 'I will just have to wait to see how the symptoms develop, I'm not going to examine you for now. Just put in an application for treatment, I will read it over and come to a decision. And I would also like to talk to your employer, just to make sure you are not a malingerer.'

The man brings all the documents and puts in an application for treatment. By this time the pains have got a whole lot worse.

The doctor says, 'Oh, it's you again – I told you it would take a bit of time. And moreover, before I can make a decision I will need to consult a professional expert. I'm only a doctor, as you know – but I can assure you that it will all be all right in the end. And by the way, your employer says that you shirk work and call in sick for no good reason.'

The man suffers, and so does his family, because he gets no diagnosis and no therapy. He continues to trust the doctor, because he still believes that the doctor knows what he is doing.

Months later the professional expert explains to him that he is a malingerer and that he does not behave like a sick person – consequently he would recommend that the doctor should continue to withhold treatment.

Deeply hurt and confused – and as a result the pain has got worse – the man just accepts the situation and waits.

Every day the man feels the pain in his chest, he can hardly work any longer. Everything feels like a strain for him, and he consults other doctors – asking why they won't examine him and give him treatment.

The other doctors all reply, 'The physician treating you knows what he is doing, and in any case he hasn't done anything wrong.'

The man goes to his doctor again. He complains about the pain being caused to him and to his family – whereupon the doctor sends him away and subjects him to penalties for 'contempt of the medical profession'. Just to be on the safe side, the man once again questions his doctor's way of proceeding, and puts in a new application for treatment of the symptoms which by this time have become almost unendurable.

The application is rejected by the doctor yet again.

The man has had enough by this time, and changes doctor. The new doctor examines the man and establishes that he has already had a number of heart attacks and that it is high time to give him treatment, but unfortunately – the new doctor says – this is not his responsibility.

The man will have to go back to his own doctor.

Four years and eight months on from his first heart attack, the man has still not been given any kind of therapy. He is practically finished, and decides to take the doctor to court for refusing him treatment, and asks the other doctors to give him their support. These again refuse their support and see no reason to make any change in their manner of proceeding. 'Your doctor,' they say, 'has done everything in proper form, and what is more he has dealt with everything in the proper time frame.'

The man just can't understand the world he is living in any more. He is entitled to therapy but he isn't getting it. They are just letting him die slowly.

But he doesn't want to die slowly, and decides to shoot himself, because life has just become unendurable for him.

When the body is found, the doctor says, 'I am not responsible for the man's death – he should have registered for examination in the proper manner and form.'

The other doctors lend him their support.

And the world still says nothing.

I will not keep silent, and will continue to make this injustice public.

Dr Robert Holzer

APPENDIX

vaeter ohne rechte

Health risks

Divorce / separation and/or loss of contact with one's own children as a health risk for men:

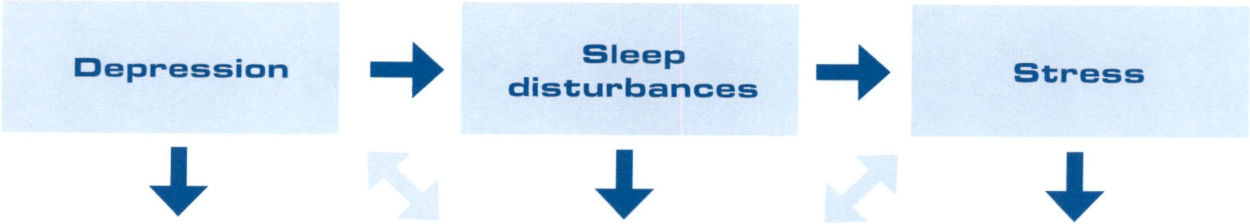

| Depression | → | Sleep disturbances | → | Stress |

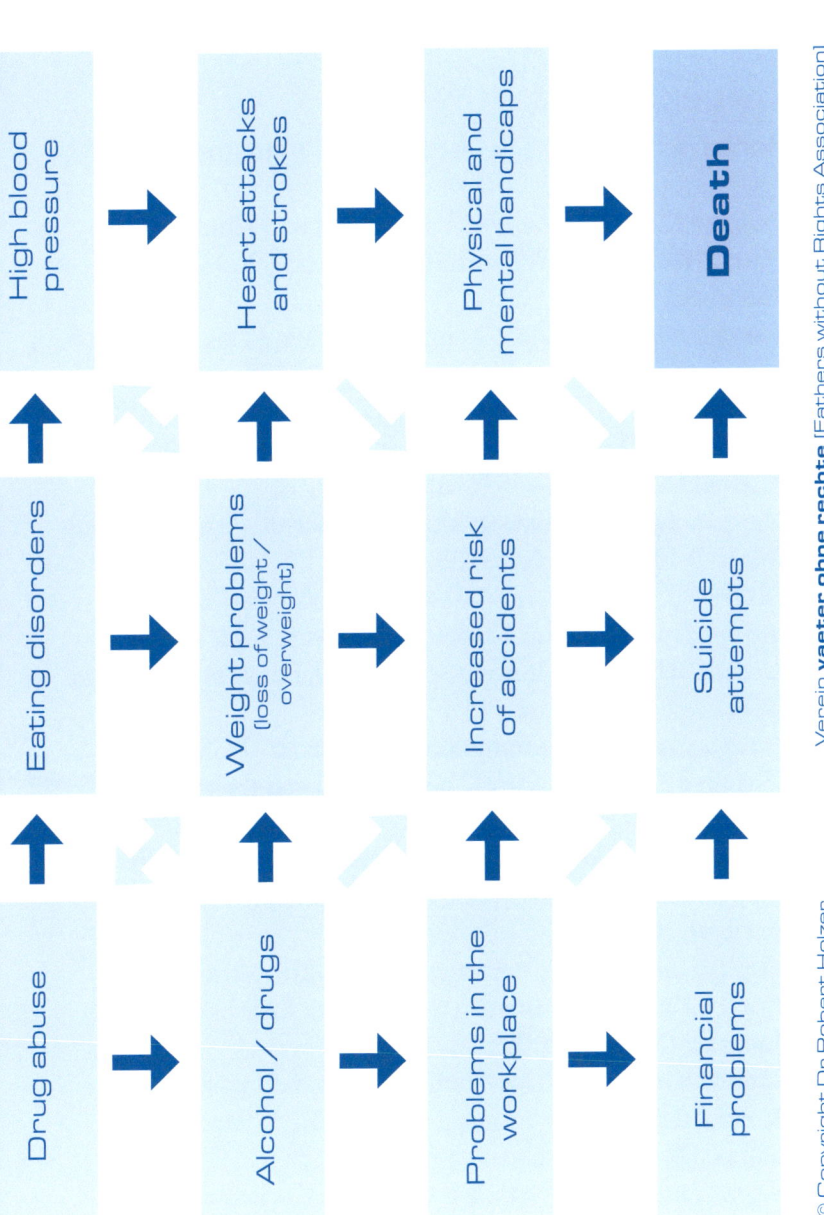

High blood pressure

Heart attacks and strokes

Physical and mental handicaps

Death

Eating disorders

Weight problems (loss of weight / overweight)

Increased risk of accidents

Suicide attempts

Drug abuse

Alcohol / drugs

Problems in the workplace

Financial problems

Bibliography

Books, associations, websites, legal fundamentals

Professor Harry Dettenborn: 'Kindeswohl und Kindeswille' ['Child Welfare and What the Child Wants'], Reinhardt Publishers, 2007

Gabriele ten Hövel: 'Liebe Mama, böser Papa / Das PAS-Syndrom' ['Nice Mum, Bad Dad – the PAS Syndrome'], Kösel Publishers, 2003

Horst Petri: 'Das Drama der Vaterentbehrung' ['The Drama of Paternal Deprivation'], Reinhardt Publishers, 2009

Matthias Matussek: 'Die vaterlose Gesellschaft' ['The Fatherless Society'], Fischer Publishers, 2006

Elisabeth Schmidt: 'Vergiss, dass es Dein Vater ist! Ehemals entfremdete Kinder im Gespräch' ['Forget that He's Your Father – Alienated Children Speak Out'], Books on Demand, 2006

Astrid v. Friesen: 'Trennungskinder klagen an!' ['Children of Separated Families Accuse!'], www.astrid-von-friesen.de

Gerald Zeiner: 'Scheidungshuren: ein Staat unterstützt die moderne Form der Prostitution' ['Divorce Whores – State Support for the Modern Form of Prostitution'], Books on Demand, 2008

Herwig Baumgartner: 'Anklage gegen Austria –Mord an unseren Kindern' ['Austria in the Dock for Child Murder'], Books on Demand, 2009

Richard A. Gardner: 'Das elterliche Entfremdungssyndrom – Parental Alienation Syndrome – PAS', Wilfrid von Boch-Galhau (WVB), 2002

Jürgen Rudolph: 'Du bist mein Kind: Die Cochemer Praxis – Wege zu einem menschlicheren Familienrecht' ['You are my

Child: the Cochem System – Paths to a more Humane Form
of Family Justice'], Schwarzkopf & Schwarzkopf, 2007
Professor Gerhard Amendt: 'Scheidungsväter: wie Väter die
Trennung von ihren Kindern erleben' ['Divorced Fathers –
how Fathers Experience Separation from their Children'],
Campus Publishers, 2006
Katrin Hummel: 'Entsorgte Väter – der Kampf um die Kinder:
Warum Männer weniger Recht bekommen' ['Fathers on the
Scrap Heap – the Battle for the Children: Why Men get a Raw
Deal' , Lübbe Publishers, 2010
Raoul Schrott: 'Das schweigende Kind' ['The Silent Child'],
Hanser Publishers, 2012
John Irving: 'Bis ich dich finde' ['Until I Find You'], Diogenes
Publishers, 2006
Humanes Recht [Humane Law]: www.humanesrecht.com
Verein Vaterverbot [Banned Fathers Association]: www.
vaterverbot.at
Verein Väter ohne Rechte [Fathers Without Rights Association]:
www.vaeter-ohne-rechte.at
Verein Doppelresidenz [Double Residence Association]: www.
doppelresidenz.at
Verein Kindergefühle [Children's Feelings Association]: www.
kindergefuehle.at
Luca Kinderschutzverein [Luca Child Protection Organisation]:
www.luca-kinderschutzverein.at

www.scheidungsindustrie.at
UN Child Rights Convention
European Human Rights Convention
European Council Treaty Series ETS 192
Austrian Federal Constitution

Allgemein Bürgerliches Recht (ABGB) [the Austrian General Civil Code]
International Covenant on Civil and Political Rights (ICCPR, 1976)

Studies on the subject of family law

Study by Professor Roland Proksch: 'Rechtstatsächliche Untersuchung zur Reform des Kindschaftsrechts' ['Investigation Based on Practical Legal Experience towards the Reform of Child Law'], Bundesanzeiger [Federal Gazette], 2002

Study by Barth-Richtarz / Figdor: 'Was bringt die gemeinsame Obsorge' ['What are the Results of Joint Custody'], study on the effects of the KindRÄG [Child Law Amendment] of 2001, commissioned by the Federal Minister of Justice, Manz, Vienna, 2008

Study by Professor Kurt Ebert: 'First call for children' , on the imperative necessity of a family law reform in Austria in keeping with the constitution and the law of nations, Innsbruck, 1995

Das parental alienation syndrome – PAS (elterliches Entfremdungssyndrom), eine interdisziplinäre Herausforderung für scheidungsbegleitende Berufe [Parental Alienation Syndrome (PAS), an Interdisciplinary Challenge to the Professions Involved in Divorce], International Conference, Frankfurt am Main, 18-19 October 2002 VWB – Verlag für Wissenschaft und Bildung [Scientific and Educational Publications], Berlin

ARGE Familienschutz [Working Consortium for Protection of the Family]: Stellungnahme zur gemeinsame Obsorge und zur Einführung des 'Kinderbeistandes' [Position Paper on Joint Custody and the Introduction of 'Separation Support for Children'], Vienna, 2009

Recommended film

Douglas Wolfsberger: 'Der entsorgte Vater' ['Father on the Scrap Heap'], DVD

About the author

Dr Robert Holzer was born in Vienna on 13.12.1963.

He is consultant in paediatrics and adolescent medicine. He is also qualified as a general practitioner and an emergency physician, and winner of the Lifesaving Medal of the City of Vienna.

Dr Robert Holzer has been an active member of various associations involved in the fathers' movement since the year 2008. Since February 2010 he has been a member of the board and press spokesman of the 'Väter ohne Rechte' ['Fathers without Rights'] association.

He is politically independent, does not belong to any party and is an Austrian citizen and tax payer without a stain on his character or record.

In August 2007 his wife of 10 years standing left him, taking the two children of the marriage (Susanne Holzer, then 9 years and 8 months of age, and Peter Holzer, then 8 years and 4 months of age) and moved to her parents in Krems an der Donau.

Both children told their father a number of times that they did not want to leave their home. Nonetheless, their mother abducted both children, taking them out of primary school and carrying them off to Krems without the knowledge and so without the consent of the father.

All the efforts of the author in approaching the Youth Welfare Office in Krems, the responsible district court of Krems and the Federal State Court of Krems, with a view to finding a solution and preventing the loss of contact between him and his beloved children, were defeated by the incapacity of the authorities and their reluctance to act, resulting in the violation of justice typical of such cases.

On the contrary, he found himself faced with every imaginable form of resistance – to the end that the children's mother should be able to enforce her ideas of the way the children should live in future without a father, deliberately bringing about Parental Alienation Syndrome.

Since 5.1.2008 he has not seen his children at all, even though joint custody was still in force and the parents were not yet divorced. On 9.12.2008, in response to the application of the woman who was still his wife, custody was withdrawn and visiting rights – which in practice had never happened – were suspended.

All this in the name of the Republic of Austria.

On 10.2.2009 the divorce applied for by his wife acquired legal effect.

In the summer of 2009, the application of the mother – now the single parent having right of custody – that the surname of the children be changed was granted by the responsible registry office in Krems. The concerns of the author (based on the 'right of hearing') in relation to this blotting out of the children's identity through the change of name, and his application that the family name be retained, were both rejected. Since then, after a period of 12 years, the children born to the marriage no longer bear his name.

In January 2011, after more than 3 years in which the author had had no contact with his children, the Federal State Court of Krems, as the court of superior jurisdiction, declared that the responsible judge of the court of the first instance had 'not been partial or dilatory'. Likewise the Public Prosecutor's Office of Korneuburg, acting on the instructions of the Public Prosecutor's Office for Cases of Corruption and the Appeals Court of the Higher Federal State Court of Vienna, having studied the relevant files for several months, rejected the charges of the author against the responsible judge in monolithic terms as being 'not sufficient grounds to accuse the judge of abuse of office' and declined to initiate proceedings. The responsible judge himself has issued a position paper in which he describes the charges against him as 'baseless'.

All applications to set a time limit between 2009 and 2011 were rejected by the Federal State Court of Krems, and the Higher Federal State Court of Vienna and the Ombudsman's Office of the Ministry of Justice are likewise of the opinion that the judge in question was 'not dilatory'. Every application for criminal proceedings to be opened against the psychological expert and the judge in question has been turned down.

In its justification of the abandonment of proceedings against the psychological expert, the Public Prosecutor's Office of Vienna states that it would be 'impossible to contemplate' that the recommendation of 'no visiting rights for the father' by a professional consultant could be detrimental to the children's welfare.

The Federal President of the Republic of Austria has declared that he has no responsibility for the issues presented by the author, and refers him to the Federal Ministry of Justice.

The second application for visiting rights of 4.5.2009 was finally implemented by the responsible judge on 1.11.2011 in the form of a court judgment ruling for NO VISITING RIGHTS (on the grounds that the children reject their father). Thus after a lapse of 2.5 years (two and a half years!) we find provisional action being taken by the court of the first instance, in the person of the judge who is deemed to be 'not partial and not dilatory'. In December 2011 the author once again appealed to the responsible federal state court against this judgment in violation of justice.

In July 2011 the responsible judge of the Federal Court of Krems recommended to the Public Prosecutor's Office of Vienna that a search of the author's house be made and his computers confiscated. Yet another proof of the attempts of the justice department to cast the author as a criminal, as a result of his strenuous opposition to the legalised abduction of his children and his revelations of the systematic and universal violations of justice in Austrian family law.

Most likely the author will be subject to the arbitrary decisions of the justice department for years to come, without any hope of the speedy implementation of the visiting rights theoretically guaranteed by the law of the land.

The names of the persons in the department of justice responsible for these breaches of the law are not given here for reasons of data protection. All original documents are in the keeping of the author and his legal representative, and are retained as documentary proof.

The author is now father on the scrap heap, reduced to being a cash cow and a mere source of income – like some 100,000 Austrian fathers, who have no contact with their children because they are prevented from doing so.

He has worked all his life for justice, equal rights and democracy, and for children's rights above all.

As a result of this legalised child abduction, testified to by the decrees of the responsible authorities in violation of basic human rights, he has lost any remaining faith in the state based on the rule of law.

His conviction of the importance and necessity of the law-based state has given way to disappointment at the meaningless way in which the written laws of the land are applied.

Acknowledgements

I would like to thank my parents, who gave me life and a childhood in which both parents were involved, and who also made it possible for me to receive an education in spite of considerable financial challenges. They will die without ever having had the chance of seeing their two grandchildren (their only grandchildren) again.

I would like in particular to thank my sister Sonja and her partner Michael, who saved me from suicide at a time when the loss of my family had made me totally desperate.

My thanks also to Edgar Neubacher, Kurt Essmann and Herwig Baumgartner, who were the first to show me that I am not alone in suffering from this unjust situation, and whose faith in justice gave me the courage to continue to fight for my children.

Likewise I would like to thank all founders and members of those associations who struggle to uphold the best interests and the rights of children who are kept apart from their fathers for no good reason. Special thanks to the founders of the 'Väter ohne Rechte' ['Fathers Without Rights'] association, Martin Stiglmayr and Martina Welz, as well as to all members of the board and supporters of the organisation.

My thanks also to Michaela Krankl and all other lawyers and specialists who have spoken out in the course of family law proceedings for the sake of our children and who, in spite of all resistance, are still trying to prevent the loss of contact between father and child.

My thanks to all mothers who do not abuse their children to gratify their own egotistical purposes and vengeful feelings or for the sake of financial reward, who do not use the children as a means to blackmail the father, and who encourage contact between father and child in spite of all the difficulties involved. They are the true guardians of child welfare, because parenthood is something that lasts lifelong – and it is the irrevocable right of the child to have the opportunity of loving both parents.

Thank you too to all friends and acquaintances who have listened to me and with whom I have found comfort.

As for all so-called friends, who quietly and unobtrusively withdrew and preferred not to speak out against legalised child abduction – may they never find themselves on the receiving end of such injustice.

'The so-called Family Law Reform of 2012 unfortunately made no difference to many of the persons affected and their children. In some cases it even made matters worse, as a result of the mandatory determination of the child's place of residence and the stipulation of a six-month trial phase to determine parental responsibilities, the latter tending to encourage alienation and the development of PAS.'